What Baby Needs

William Sears, M.D., Martha Sears, R.N.,
and Christie Watts Kelly

Illustrated by Renée Andriani

LITTLE, BROWN AND COMPANY
New York   Boston

To our children who now have children and who are showing us how
parenting really is a long-term investment
—W. S. and M.S.

To my beautiful children, Arabella and Patrick Graham,
for teaching me that love truly multiplies with each new member of the family
—C. W. K.

For Ellen, Joe, and Maggie; with all my love
—R. A.

Text copyright © 2004 by William Sears, Martha Sears, and Christie Watts Kelly
Illustrations copyright © 2001 by Renée Andriani

Little, Brown and Company

Hachette Book Group
237 Park Avenue, New York, NY 10017
Visit our website at www.lb-kids.com

Little, Brown and Company is a division of Hachette Book Group, Inc.
The Little, Brown name and logo are trademarks of Hachette Book Group, Inc.

First Edition: September 2001

Library of Congress Cataloging-in-Publication Data

Sears, William, M.D.
    What baby needs / by William Sears and Martha Sears, with Christie Watts Kelly ; illustrated by Renée Andriani.—1st ed.
        p. cm.
    Includes bibliographical references.
    ISBN 978-0-316-78828-1
    1. Infants (Newborn)—Care—Juvenile literature.[1 Babies.] I. Sears, Martha. II. Kelly.
Christie Watts. III. Williams-Andriani, Renée, ill. IV. Title
    HQ774.S453   2000
    649'.122—dc21
                                                                            00-037529

10 9 8 7

TWP

NOTES FOR PARENTS AND CAREGIVERS

Parents and caregivers will find it helpful to preview this book and read these notes before sharing the book with a child. The text and illustrations reflect a responsive parenting style known as Attachment Parenting. (See "About Attachment Parenting" on page 32.)

🐾 Since baby feeding and sleeping choices are very individual, we encourage you to modify the text as you read to your child, according to the choices you make in your family.

🐾 When describing bodily functions such as breastfeeding, use the words you feel most comfortable using.

🐾 Even if an older sibling has been weaned for quite some time, he or she may ask to nurse. Typically, the best approach is to allow the child to try it once or twice, and then he or she will lose interest. If the child is younger, recently weaned, and you both want to resume nursing, contact La Leche League (see "Resources" on page 32) for information on tandem nursing.

🐾 Having a new baby in the home can bring up a wide range of feelings for an older child. The "What About Me?" sidebars will help you understand and validate your child's experiences and emotions.

🐾 Children are often eager to play with the new baby — and often find it difficult to wait until the baby will be able to play like an older child. The "Making Friends with Your Baby" sidebars give ideas of ways to foster meaningful interaction between your children.

🐾 To focus on the older child's new status as an older brother or sister, consider having the child help you make and send out "older brother" or "older sister" announcements along with (or instead of) baby announcements. Perhaps make a special "sibling book" with side-by-side pictures of each child.

🐾 For the weeks and months after the baby arrives, keep a stash of simple, wrapped gifts to dole out to the older child when visitors bring a gift for the baby (don't forget to allow the older child to open gifts brought for the baby, as well). Have another stash of simple activity toys such as crayons, puzzles, and cassette tapes handy to help entertain the older child on those tough days when the baby is demanding a lot of attention (although you don't want to make a habit of replacing your attention with material possessions).

🐾 Many times, well-meaning adults overuse the "big brother/big sister" or "big boy/big girl" language. From the child's perspective, all the advantage seems to be in being little — after all, the baby gets more attention and never makes mistakes. Try to use the term "older brother" or "older sister," to more accurately reflect the child's new role. On the other hand, most kids will proudly wear the badge of "big helper," as that emphasizes their ability to be a vital member of the family community.

🐾 Never leave an infant alone in a room with a young sibling. It only takes a second for something to happen — for the older child to poke the baby's eyes or to pinch, hit, or drop the baby. You're not only protecting the infant, but the older child as well — if they find out they have that much power it will be scary to them. And if anything bad does happen, the older child will feel terribly guilty later on. Also beware of the older child hugging or squeezing the baby too hard — either because the older child doesn't know better, or as a way of being aggressive in a seemingly acceptable manner.

🐾 Don't let fear of hurting your older child's feelings interfere with forming a loving connection with your new baby. Except in emergency situations, a young baby's needs must always come first. An older sibling whose own needs were met as an infant will have a much easier time handling any frustration that crops up.

🐾 It is important to allow children to express their frustration or other "negative" feelings without invalidating them. For example, if the child says something like, "I hate the baby," don't negate that feeling by saying, "No, you don't, you love the baby." Instead, try saying something like, "It's hard for you to see Mommy spending so much time with the baby." Once the child's feelings are validated, then the intensity of the feelings tends to dissipate.

When your family has a new baby,
you are growing up, becoming an
older brother or older sister.

You are Mommy and Daddy's "big helper," and you're
learning just what your baby needs — the very same
things you needed when you were a little baby.

WHAT ABOUT ME?

🐾 Ask your mommy and daddy to show you your baby book and pictures of when you were a tiny baby. See if you can find pictures of yourself right after you were born, being nursed by your mommy, sleeping, being held, and crying.

Just like you did when you were a baby, the new baby needs to be with a family right from the start. That's why you and your mommy and daddy hold your baby skin-to-skin,

snuggle with your baby nose-to-nose,

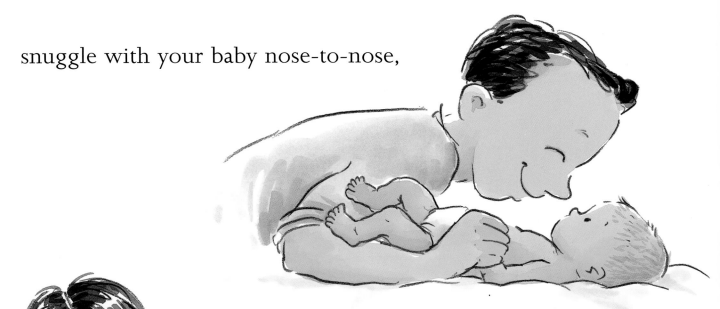

and count your baby's tiny fingers
and curled-up toes.

Just like you did, Baby needs to eat. Very, very often, day and night. Babies have tiny tummies that like one thing best — their mommies' milk. That's why Baby nurses to get milk from your mommy's breasts.

Or, when Baby is older,
Baby might be fed Mommy's milk
from a bottle if Mommy has to be away.

Baby needs to sleep, too. But Baby has been close to Mommy's heartbeat and feels lonely to be far away from it.

That's why Baby likes to sleep close by Mommy,
just like you did when you were little.

And just like you did, Baby needs to be held. Baby feels safe and cozy watching the world from Mommy's or Daddy's arms or from inside a baby carrier.

And Baby likes to sit in your lap and
be held by you, too, with a little help
from Mommy and Daddy.

Just like you did, Baby needs to cry. Crying is the way tiny babies can talk, the way they can show us what they really need. Babies cry because they're hungry, tired, lonely, or even because they need a clean diaper.

The sooner someone helps a crying baby, the sooner the baby will stop crying.

When you were a little baby, your family and friends formed a circle of love to welcome you into the world — and now your family's new baby will become a part of that same circle of love.

Now you're growing up, and you can
do lots of things that little babies can't
do. You can go play at a friend's house.

You can eat ice cream.

And you can ride a tricycle.

You can do fun things with Daddy,
too, like go to the park.

When Mommy is feeding the baby, you can snuggle up right next to her and read a book, you can take care of your own little baby doll, or you can have some "just-being time" with Mommy.

MAKING FRIENDS WITH YOUR BABY

🍼 Babies need lots of sleep to keep from feeling grumpy. Never wake a sleeping baby on purpose.

🍼 Sit and hold your baby brother or sister very gently in your lap. *Always* have an adult help you.

🍼 Gently touch the inside of Baby's hand with your finger, and Baby will squeeze your finger.

When Mommy takes Baby to the doctor for a checkup, you can see how Baby is growing up just like you. And maybe the doctor will check to see how strong and healthy you are, too.

See how you GROW!

MAKING FRIENDS WITH YOUR BABY

🐛 Make silly faces and funny noises (not too loud!), and see if Baby will smile at you.

🐛 Learn how to help change Baby's diaper and help give Baby a bath.

🐛 Read your favorite book to Baby.

When Mommy goes to the grocery store, the gas station, or the library, you can help her by quickly buckling your seat belt when you get into the car,

by talking and singing to the baby,
and by staying close by
Mommy and Baby all the time.

It might seem like whenever you see Mommy, the baby is with her, too. But it won't always be that way. Sometimes Daddy will hold the baby, and you can have special time with Mommy.

WHAT ABOUT ME?

Sometimes you might wish the baby could go live somewhere else, or you might feel sad or angry at the baby, and that's okay. Tell your mommy and daddy how you feel. It's okay to hit a pillow, but you must never, ever hurt the baby.

And, before you know it, the baby
will hold your hand . . .

smile at you . . .

sit up . . .

and play!

About Attachment Parenting

Attachment parenting is a *responsive* style of parenting that helps facilitate a child's secure emotional attachments. When parents understand, anticipate, and meet their children's needs in a developmentally appropriate way, they establish a warm, connected relationship based on love and trust.

Connectedness, love, and *trust* — but not permissiveness — are keys to the attachment parenting concept of discipline. When parents model desirable behavior and set boundaries and consequences based on readiness, children tend to behave appropriately out of a desire to please rather than from fear of punishment.

Attachment parenting is an *approach,* rather than a strict set of rules. It's the way many people parent instinctively — comforting a crying baby, showing an older child a constructive way to vent frustrations, guiding children to independence by providing a secure base. The following "Five Baby Bs" are attachment parenting tools that can help parents and babies get connected right from the start.

1. Birth bonding: Babies need to continue feeling connected after birth, no matter what kind of birth situation. Planning ahead to allow skin-to-skin contact with mom and dad, breastfeeding, and rooming-in with your baby if at the hospital will set the stage for a good start to the parenting relationship.

2. Breastfeeding: Human milk is the best food for baby humans. Breastfeeding as soon as possible after birth gives the optimal chance for a good start. Continuing as long as possible helps both baby and parents reap the most benefits.

3. Babywearing: Carried babies are more content and less fussy, giving them more quiet and alert time for cognitive and physical development. Being physically close to baby helps parents learn to read baby's signals and develop intuition about baby's needs.

4. Being flexible in sleeping arrangements: Babies need to be close to parents at night as well as the daytime. Co-sleeping (sleeping in the same bed or the same room) can be an effective way to satisfy a baby's needs as well as to make life easier for a nursing mother. It also helps working parents reconnect with their children after being separated all day.

5. Belief in the language value of a baby's cry (and other cues): Since infants can't talk, their only means of communication are through body language and crying. Parents learn to read their baby's body language and pre-cry signals as well as their cries — and respond appropriately to the baby's needs, helping baby develop trust and communication skills.

Resources

www.askdrsears.com is an interactive Web site where you can ask — and find the answers to — your toughest parenting questions.

www.parenting.com features articles by William and Martha Sears.

The Sears Parenting Library, by William Sears, M.D., and Martha Sears, R.N.

The Pregnancy Book: Everything You Need to Know from America's Baby Experts, written with Linda Hughey Holt, M.D., F.A.C.O.G.

The Birth Book: Everything You Need to Know to Have a Safe and Satisfying Birth

The Breastfeeding Book: Everything You Need to Know About Nursing Your Child From Birth Through Weaning

The Baby Book: Everything You Need to Know About Your Baby — From Birth to Age Two

The Fussy Baby Book: Everything You Need to Know — From Birth to Age Five

The Discipline Book: Everything You Need to Know to Have a Better-Behaved Child — From Birth to Age Ten

The Family Nutrition Book: Everything You Need to Know About Feeding Your Children — From Birth Through Adolescence

The A.D.D. Book: New Understandings, New Approaches to Parenting Your Child, written with Lynda Thompson, Ph.D.

Attachment Parenting International (API) is a member organization networking with attachment parents, professionals, and like-minded organizations around the world. In addition to parent support groups, the organization provides educational and research materials. 1508 Clairmont Place, Nashville, TN 37215, USA; www.attachmentparenting.org; 615-298-4334.

La Leche League International (LLLI) is the world's foremost authority on breastfeeding, offering breastfeeding support groups in cities worldwide, one-on-one help for breastfeeding mothers, and a catalog of products and literature. 1400 North Meacham Road, Schaumburg, IL 60173-4048, USA; www.lalecheleague.org; 847-519-7730; 800-LA-LECHE (525-3243).